Will Burtin
The Display of
Visual Knowledge

BY R. ROGER REMINGTON

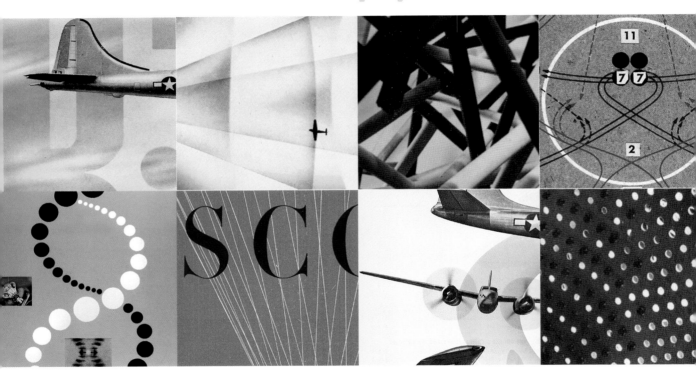

BURTIN

Will Burtin
The Display of
Visual Knowledge

BY R. ROGER REMINGTON

GRAPHIC DESIGN ARCHIVES
CHAPBOOK SERIES: THREE

RIT
CARY GRAPHIC ARTS PRESS
2009

Will Burtin
The Display of
Visual Knowledge

BY R. ROGER REMINGTON

GRAPHIC DESIGN ARCHIVES
CHAPBOOK SERIES: THREE

RIT
CARY GRAPHIC ARTS PRESS
90 Lomb Memorial Drive
Rochester, New York 14623-5604
http://carypress.rit.edu

Copyright ©2009 Rochester Institute of Technology,
RIT Cary Graphic Arts Press and R. Roger Remington

Unless otherwise credited, all illustrations are used with permission of the
Will Burtin Collection, Archives and Special Collections, RIT Libraries,
Rochester Institute of Technology, with thanks and appreciation to
Carol Burtin Fripp and Robert S. P. Fripp. Every reasonable effort has been
made to contact copyright holders of materials reproduced in this book.

FRONT COVER: *Portrait of Will Burtin.* Used by permission of Pfizer, Inc.
Handwritten script of Will Burtin. Used by permission of Carol Burtin Fripp
BACK COVER: *Will Burtin at his desk in 1971.* Portrait ©A.V. Sobolewski
INSIDE COVERS: *Photo by Jerry Cooke.* ©The Jerry Cooke Archives, Inc.

ISBN 978-1-933360-36-2 Printed in USA

Library of Congress Cataloging-in-Publication Data

Remington, R. Roger.
    Will Burtin: the display of visual knowledge/by R. Roger Remington.
        p. cm.–(Graphic design archives chapbook series; 3)
    Includes bibliographical references.
    ISBN 978-1-933360-36-2 (alk. paper)
    1. Burtin, Will, 1908–1972–Criticism and interpretation.
    2. Graphic design (Typography)–United States–History–20th century.
    3. Commercial art–United States–History–20th century. I. Title.
        NC999.4.B87R47 2009
        741.6092–dc22

                2008052120

Will Burtin

From the catalog
Fifty Years AIGA Exhibition
1966
Champion Papers, Inc.

The last fifty years brought a continuous acceleration in the growth of scientific knowledge. The technological-social consequences of applied sciences affect everybody by what we do with them and what they do to our future. Potential aspects of nuclear power permit only two human choices: to improve morally or to perish. From now on all deeds and thought cannot avoid evaluation as to which of the two they favor. Ours then, is an age of great peril, but of even greater opportunities. Communications have a vital function in this transformation of values. Visual design—including advertising—must assist in the continuous education for improvement. Creative arts can only benefit from embracing the new manifestations and profound human meanings of scientific insight, which they need for the comprehensive construction of a world culture.

FOREWORD

Amy Vilz
Getty Project Archivist
for the Will Burtin Collection
2005–2006

THE GRAPHIC DESIGN ARCHIVES AT ROCHESTER INSTITUTE OF Technology includes several influential graphic designers of the twentieth century. The companion chapbook series has previously studied two of these pioneering designers, Lester Beall and Cipe Pineles. The third chapbook in this series continues with an exploration of *Will Burtin: The Display of Visual Knowledge*.

Will Burtin (1908–1972) was part of a revolutionary group of mid-century graphic designers that included Paul Rand, Lester Beall, and Alvin Lustig who changed the way in which information was transmitted to the public—be it through advertising, popular magazines, or technical information. In 1948, Burtin's exhibit *Integration: The New Discipline in Design*, opened at the Composing Room in New York City. In the introduction to the exhibition, designer Serge Chermayeff stated:

> "This new art of 'visualization,' of giving visual form in two or three dimensions to a message... is the product of a new kind of artist functionary evolved by our complex society. This artist possesses the inclusive equipment of liberal knowledge, scientific and technical experience, and artistic ability... Among the small band of pioneers who have developed this new language by bringing patient research and brilliant inventiveness to their task is Will Burtin."[1]

1 *Integration* exhibition booklet
  1949, pp. 2, folder 55.6, Will Burtin Papers
  RIT Libraries: Graphic Design Archives
  Rochester Institute of Technology

Vision 65 Conference poster
In October 1965, 27 speakers addressed
490 delegates at Southern Illinois University

Atomic Energy in Action Exhibit
Photograph by Ezra Stoller © Esto

Designer, visionary, and teacher, Burtin's innovations can be seen in the variety of work he produced throughout his career. His tenure as art director of *Fortune* magazine (1945–1949) was marked by his seemingly effortless illustrative layouts, distilling complicated information into comprehensive visual terms.

Burtin's integrative approach and commitment to design is also apparent in his participation and organization of several ground-breaking conferences, including the *International Design Conference at Aspen* series, *1958 Art and Science of Typography* at Silvermine, *Vision 65*, and *Vision 67*. These symposia brought together designers and typographers, as well as scientists, writers, educators, and artists in the spirit of collaboration and communication in the advancement of modern design.

Will Burtin is best known for his large-scale exhibits that were "walk-in" style displays. They were immensely popular, enveloping visitors within the size of the construction and the scope of its content. One of the most successful of the exhibits was produced for the United States Information Agency, *Kalamazoo… and how it grew!* (1958), which was a depiction of life in a characteristic mid-western town.

Portraying the complexities of atomic energy, Burtin designed *The Atom in Action* (1962), showcased at Union Carbide's headquarters in New York City. New construction techniques and a unique "flying carpet" design brought considerable attention to Burtin's *Eastman Kodak Pavilion* at the 1964–65 World's Fair.

SCOPE

Most noteworthy, Burtin worked for 22 years for the Upjohn Company, a giant in the pharmaceutical world where he served as both design consultant and art director of Upjohn's publication, *Scope*. His work on *Scope* exemplified his use of graphics and imagery in communicating complicated journal text. Burtin was instrumental in the development of the expression of a cohesive corporate identity for Upjohn, a new concept in the advertising world. During this time, he also produced some of the most distinguished and novel exhibits of his career: the *Cell* (1958), the *Brain* (1960), and *Inflammation: Defense of Life* (1969). Once again, Burtin's hallmark was employing the unique ability to visually express complex concepts in a sophisticated yet aesthetically pleasing and accessible manner. This style emerged as the defining characteristic of Burtin's work.

This chapbook, as well as the materials found in the Will Burtin Collection in the Graphic Design Archives, can be studied to give meaningful understanding to Burtin's design process. The papers include voluminous correspondence regarding projects, as well as notes, publications, artwork, films, architectural drawings, audio materials, exhibit models, and photographs, many taken by Burtin's close friend, Ezra Stoller.

Upjohn

**Will Burtin, on leave
with daughter Carol Burtin**
1943, Photograph by Hilda Burtin
Courtesy of Carol Burtin Fripp

A special thank you is extended to Carol Burtin Fripp for donating the Burtin Collection and entrusting her father's legacy to the Graphic Design Archives at Rochester Institute of Technology. I thank Vignelli Professor R. Roger Remington for his tireless support of the Design Archives and his insightful work on Will Burtin. I am also appreciative to the Getty Foundation for its generous funding to process the Will Burtin Collection, and those that contributed include: Kari Horowicz, CIAS librarian and editor of the chapbook series, Rebecca Simmons, Jody Sidlauskas, Anna Kuipers, Lindsay Sidlauskas, and Sara Tkac—it was an honor to work with you and be a part of the project. Lastly, thanks to Professor Bruce Ian Meader, book designer and the staff of the Cary Graphic Arts Press, David Pankow, Amelia Hugill-Fontanel, Molly Cort, and Marnie Soom. I have no doubt your approach to design and attention to detail would be most appreciated by Will Burtin.

**Will Burtin and colleagues,
U.S. Army, Office of
Strategic Services, 1943**
Courtesy of Will Burtin Collection, RIT

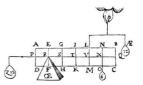

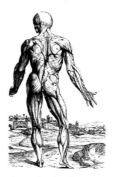

Will Burtin at his desk in 1971
Portrait © A. V. Sobolewski

Illustration by Simon Stevin
Courtesy of Professor Krzysztof Lenk

The Ninth Plate of the Muscles Plate 32
Illustration from the Works of Andreas Vesalius of Brussels
J. B. deC. M. Saunders and Charles D. O'Malley
Dover Publications, Inc. New York, 1950

Will Burtin
The Display of Visual Knowledge
BY R. ROGER REMINGTON

Visualizing the Invisible

From the dawn of history, humans have been curious about those aspects of life that are beyond our limited human perceptual and cognitive capabilities. Bill Bryson, in his popular book *A Short History of Nearly Everything*, wrote:

> "Most of the real diversity in evolution has been small-scale. We large things are just flukes—an interesting side branch. Of the twenty-three main divisions of life, only three—plants, animals and fungi—are large enough to be seen by the human eye, and even they contain species that are microscopic.... The world belongs to the very small—and it has for a very long time."[1]

1 Bill Bryson
  A Short History of Nearly Everything
  New York: Broadway Books, 2003
  pp. 311–12

The need to document and visualize the invisible in order to understand it has been an intellectual and indeed, even a spiritual quest. Historical evidence of this eternal inquiry abounds, including the Lascaux cave paintings, Chinese Chia-ku-wen writing, Native American pictographs, the earliest printed books, Stevin's sixteenth-century illustrated mechanical diagrams, Leeuwenhoek's magnifying lenses, the anatomical drawings of Vesalius and da Vinci, Röntgen's first x-ray image, the electron microscope revealing sub-atomic particles, and today's diagnostic diffusion tensor imaging.

2 Andrew Pollack
Custom-Made Microbes at Your Service:
Life Imitating Art
New York Times, January 17, 2006
p. F1

3 *Bodies: The Exhibition*, advertisement
New York Times, January 17, 2006
p. F1

4 Jim Foley and Bill Ribarsky
Next-Generation Data Visualization Tools
Scientific Visualization Advances and
Challenges, New York: Academic Press, 1994
p. 104

5 Marla Schweppe
in discussion with the author
interview January, 2006

Recently, a national newspaper feature story on science explained in text and diagram how scientists are now manufacturing whole colonies of genetically modified bacteria in a way in which they become compatible.[2] The next page in the same issue carried an advertisement for *Bodies: The Exhibition*, a touring show of human cadavers which had been preserved through an innovative process before being put on display. The ad states, "Experience the human body like never before when you visit Bodies."[3] These events remind us of how mankind constantly seeks to better understand our world and how the manifestation of this curiosity is so dominant and important in our daily lives. We want to know how we got here, how our bodies work, and how the world around us operates. This curiosity seems to be present in every profession, from graphic design to medicine to information technology.

The Disciplines of Visualization
The term visualization has many meanings and is associated with numerous contemporary disciplines ranging from information technology to psychology to graphic design; others in even more disparate fields have also claimed ownership of the word. The 1966 edition of the *Random House Dictionary of the English Language* defines it as "to make perceptible to the mind or imagination."

In 1994, scientists Foley and Ribarsky suggested that visualization meant "mapping" representations that can be perceived.[4] Marla Schweppe, an RIT professor, provides a simple meaning by saying that visualization refers to "making information and ideas visual."[5] In this digital age, the author's definition is that visualization is a tool or method for interpreting image data fed into a computer and for generating images from complex multi-dimensional data sets.

Will Burtin as a young man
Photograph by Hilda Burtin
10 x 9 inches
Courtesy of Carol Burtin Fripp

6 Will Burtin
    Design and Communication
    Education of Vision
    edited by Gyorgy Kepes
    New York: George Braziller, Inc, 1965
    p. 78

Within the context of today's "information explosion," designers often categorize the visual exploration of invisible processes as a subset of information design, and call it "visualization." In this essay, visualization will be discussed in relation to the area of graphic and information design.

Will Burtin, a Modernist Designer
The designer Will Burtin (1908–1972) himself provided the most useful characterization of visualization: "Communication designers may be destined to play a vital role in the future, because it is the essential function of their profession in our society to enhance and cultivate communications toward easier understanding of ideas and complex problems, in the shortest possible time and higher visual and auditory retention of data."[6]

Burtin, a pioneering graphic designer who greatly advanced the practice of visualization, was influenced by the European avant-garde artists and designers. He was trained as a typographer in Germany and immigrated to the United States in 1938. During World War II, he worked with the United States Office of Strategic Services to design highly visual training manuals for gunners to use while in flight. After the war, he became the art director at *Fortune* magazine, and in this capacity applied his interest in visualization to the development of charts and diagrams that the magazine regularly featured to help businessmen understand complex processes in manufacturing and science. By 1950, he had begun his own design firm and created exemplary work for many clients such as Union Carbide, Eastman Kodak, and the Smithsonian Institution. However, his major client for most of his career was the Upjohn Company, a drug manufacturer based in Kalamazoo, Michigan.

Scope magazine cover
Volume V, No. 2, 1957
Used by permission of Pfizer, Inc.

7 Will Burtin
  Untitled writings, Will Burtin Collection
  Archives and Special Collections
  Wallace Library
  Rochester Institute of Technology
  Rochester, New York

In his projects for Upjohn, Burtin became obsessed with the visual aspects of science. He created five major interpretive exhibits for the company, including The *Cell* in 1958 and The *Brain* in 1960. He also designed *Scope*, Upjohn's magazine for health professionals, and for those readers, as he did for *Fortune*'s, he often included charts and diagrams to make content about physiology and pharmaceuticals clear and comprehensible.

Burtin's approach to visualization was grounded in his life-long career focus on functionalism in design. Whether in advertising, exhibits, magazines, or other print material, his constant goal was to provide the audience with optimum communication of the content. He sought in every project, whether simple or complex, to make whatever he created understandable to the viewer. Burtin understood that, "Information is power. Conveying information is conveying power to people, empowering them."[7] He wanted to be remembered as a communicator—and also believed strongly that if people are given good design they will choose it over bad design.

Visualization in Application

An effective way of bringing clarity and meaning to visualization is through examples. What follows are historic case studies of two major projects from Will Burtin's career: a set of military manuals designed during World War II, and from 15 years later, a landmark exhibition commissioned by the Upjohn Company.

Gunnery in the A-26
November, 1944, Air Force Manual No. 56

Harmonization of the A-26
December, 1944, Section A601
in Gunnery in the A-26 Manual
United States Air Force

Gunnery Manuals for the United States Army Air Corps

During World War II Burtin was employed as a designer for the Training Aids Division of the Office of Strategic Services. Among other assignments, he and a colleague, the writer Lawrence P. Lessing (1908–1990), created four training manuals for personnel in the u. s. Army Air Corps, including *Gunnery in the A-26* and the *Gunners' Information File: Flexible Gunnery*, both produced in 1944. Burtin and Lessing were assisted by Max Gschwind (1894–1984), an illustrator with an extraordinary ability to visualize technical processes.

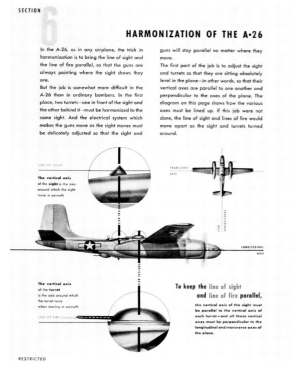

Position Firing manual covers
Section of the Gunner's Information File
Air Force Manual No. 20, pp. S-14–S-15
United States Air Force

Burtin wrote that when given the assignment, "I did quite a bit of flying and studying about flying in the meantime and the job— a manual for the Air Corps—is getting along fast now. There are so amazingly many problems involved that it is not surprising that pilots and aerial gunners need between 8 and 13 months until they are ready to face the final test: Combat."[8]

Each gunner had to learn his gun's mechanism inside out in the shortest possible time. Consequently, the message had to be direct and swiftly to the point. A movie was considered for this purpose, but tests proved that movies had poor memory value in terms of detail, even in repeated showings. Therefore, a loose-leaf manual form was chosen, retaining as much as possible of the cinematic techniques…. Photographs were silhouetted so as to bring out detail and interpose no square halftone blocks in the visual stream. Titles were pulled out of the text blocks, set bold to facilitate an easy visual grasp of the subject, but set no larger than the body type to avoid disrupting in the sequence of operations.[9]

The aerial gunner had to be taught a method for measuring off gun deflections against a fighter plane attacking his own bomber, in which the gunner had to judge the correct angle of the fighter's attack, its duration, and allow for the fighter's motion and the speed of his own bomber. [10]

8 Will Burtin
Letter to A. Garrard MacLeod
January 9, 1944, Will Burtin Collection
Archives and Special Collections
Wallace Library
Rochester Institute of Technology
Rochester, New York

9 Will Burtin and L. P. Lessing
Interrelations, Graphis 4, No. 22
January 9, 1948, p. 108

10 Ibid, 109

Position Firing manual
Section of the Gunner's Information File
Air Force Manual No. 20, pp. S-14–S-15
United States Air Force

11 Ibid, p. 109

To create an understanding of this space-time-motion relationship, Burtin approached the problem in three steps:

1 First, the area around the bomber was laid out on a one-dimensional plane using color to illuminate its basic measurements.

2 Then the one-dimensional changed into the three-dimensional by the projection of imaginary, transparent cones in space.

3 Finally, the gunner was shown how the angle measurements of these cones were carried forward and backward in space and measured with the rings of his gun-sight.[11]

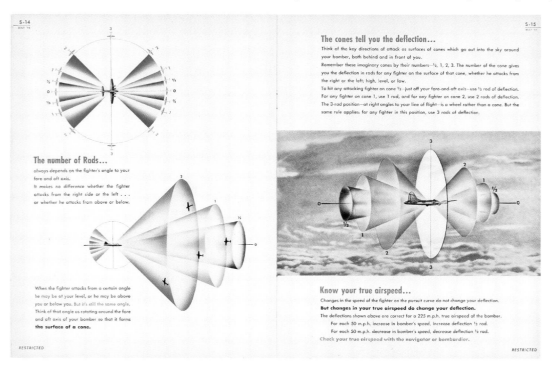

The number of Rads...
always depends on the fighter's angle to your fore and aft axis.
It makes no difference whether the fighter attacks from the right side or the left . . . or whether he attacks from above or below.

When the fighter attacks from a certain angle he may be at your level, or he may be above you or below you. But it's still the same angle. Think of that angle as rotating around the fore and aft axis of your bomber so that it forms **the surface of a cone.**

The cones tell you the deflection...
Think of the key directions of attack as surfaces of cones which go out into the sky around your bomber, both behind and in front of you.
Remember these imaginary cones by their numbers—½, 1, 2, 3. The number of the cone gives you the deflection in rads for any fighter on the surface of that cone, whether he attacks from the right or the left; high, level, or low.
To hit any attacking fighter on cone ½—just off your fore-and-aft axis—use ½ rad of deflection. For any fighter on cone 1, use 1 rad, and for any fighter on cone 2, use 2 rads of deflection. The 3-rad position—at right angles to your line of flight—is a wheel rather than a cone. But the same rule applies: for any fighter in this position, use 3 rads of deflection.

Know your true airspeed...
Changes in the speed of the fighter on the pursuit curve do not change your deflection.
But changes in your true airspeed do change your deflection.
The deflections shown above are correct for a 225 m.p.h. true airspeed of the bomber.
For each 50 m.p.h. increase in bomber's speed, increase deflection ½ rad.
For each 50 m.p.h. decrease in bomber's speed, decrease deflection ½ rad.
Check your true airspeed with the navigator or bombardier.

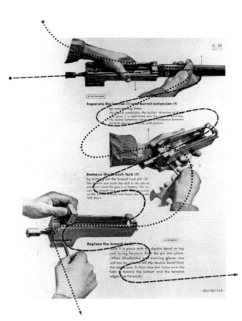

This is your Gun:
The Caliber 50
Browning Machine Gun
M2 Aircraft Basic
Used by permission from
Graphis *22, 1948, p. 108*

At this time Burtin wrote, "Graphic presentation now provides the visual tools for making coherent a world of steadily enlarging and refining dimensions."[12] These manual pages remain as exemplars of information design at its finest, and attest to Burtin's passion for clear communication.

In 1948, Burtin and Lessing looked back on their wartime design work and wrote about it for the magazine *Graphis*. To illustrate his points, Burtin showed pages from one of the training manuals, on which he overlaid directional lines to indicate the route by which readers would follow the information flow. The "dotted line roughly indicates the path of the eye in its first, quick comprehensive glance over the page. The flow line oscillates left to right to accommodate Western eyes long trained in that direction. The dotted line follows the eye's subsequent return to the page for close reading and detailed study of its contents. All manual pages were designed to allow for both forms of optical comprehension."[13]

In an era long before the word "visualization" was coined, Burtin saw the need for functional graphics and understood their importance in simplifying complex ideas. In that pre-digital era, he felt that designers had the visual tools at hand for creating coherent representations in a steadily enlarging world.

12 Ibid, p. 108

13 Ibid, 108

14 Ibid, 109

Of the gunners' manuals he wrote, "As happens whenever all
the elements of a design are recognized, studied, and brought
coherently together, the result is hardly ever unpleasing to the
eye—indeed, it achieves a certain beauty of clear statement—
and it is effective in its purpose."[14] And the manuals indeed served
their intended purpose: their use shortened the training time
for aerial gunners from twelve weeks to six weeks thus, through
visualization, Burtin effectively made a significant contribution
to the Allied war effort.

**Electrical System
Turret Operation Diagram**
Gunnery in the A-26 Manual
United States Air Force

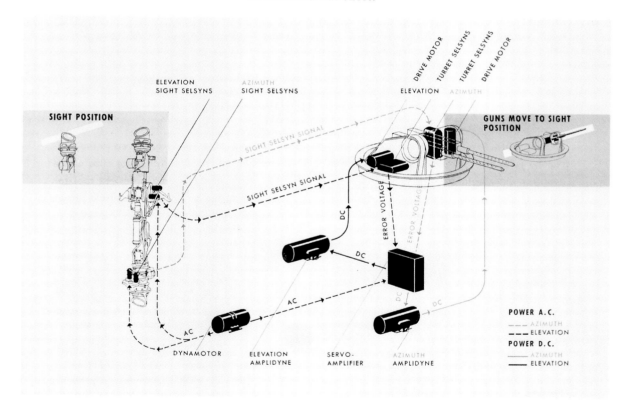

**The *Cell*: An Exhibit Presenting
the Basic Unit of the Life**
1959, Kalamazoo, Michigan
Exhibition catalog, The Upjohn Company
Used by permission of Pfizer, Inc.

**Will Burtin examining a portion
of The *Cell* Exhibit** *Left*
c. 1958–1959
Photograph by Ezra Stoller © Esto
8 x 10 inches

15 Will Burtin
    Integration: The New Discipline in Design
    New York: A-D Gallery, 1948
    Sponsored by the Composing Room
    unpaginated, p. 22

16 Will Burtin
    Untitled writings, essay, 1948
    Will Burtin Collection
    Archives and Special Collections
    Wallace Library
    Rochester Institute of Technology
    Rochester, New York

The Cell Exhibit for the Upjohn Company, 1958

Burtin's career exemplified the power of graphic design in translating the complex, largely invisible world of science into a clear, visible reality that could be understood and remembered. He stated his visionary mission in a 1948 exhibit brochure, "With patience and further study, we will ultimately succeed in making our methods of visual organization more precise and the designer's unparalleled opportunity for integrating the elements of our society, clearer to himself and to the world."[15]

The approach of taking highly technical scientific data and translating it into clear information was particularly evident in all aspects of Burtin's work for Upjohn, from print and collateral materials to advertising, packaging, and corporate identity. The most unique Upjohn projects, however, were the series of visionary public exhibits which Burtin called "exhibit sculpture." Of them, he wrote, "It occured [sic] to me that three-dimensional exhibit structures could be useful in establishing a physical and orderly relationship of relevant data. Such devices should be frankly educational, would be a public service and a credit to Upjohn, thereby helping their business efforts as well."[16]

As a first step, Burtin proposed to create for the company a communications program that would present the visual structure of a cell in three dimensions. In an essay written in preparation for the project's design implementation, Burtin wrote, "Prior interest in cytology and study of cell information had shown that many research activities around the world had separated this tiny universe into so many different fields and uninitiated and even medically-trained people could no longer get a clear impression even about the main results of research, let alone trends and speculative ideas.

**Will Burtin showing plastic tubing
to visitors inside The *Cell* Exhibit**

c. 1959, Photograph by Ezra Stoller © Esto
10 x 8 inches

It was quite certain that a coherent visual presentation—a model—would be in the general interest and of considerable educational value. The Client concurred with this objective." [17]

It was Burtin's belief that scientific communication models must have three essential qualifications:

First: the model must enhance a feeling for—and not distort understanding of—the reality behind the communication by limiting its contents to clearly apparent objectives.

Second: the design analysis of the model must be motivated by a devotion to clarity to assure that its three-dimensional form is the most economical, time-saving and meaningful way to convey the information.

Third: organization and translation of data into space, scale, material, form, color motion, sound or timed sequence must result in such a simple and yet intense sensory and logically structured experience that the model is easy to remember. [18]

17 Ibid

18 Will Burtin
   *Thoughts on Three-Dimensional
   Science Communications*
   Dot Zero, 4
   Summer, 1967, No. 4, pp. 30–31

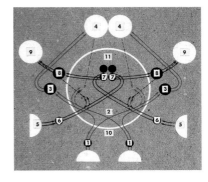

**Will Burtin's
visual diagram
for the Upjohn
Brain Exhibit**

c. 1960
*Used by permission
of Pfizer, Inc.*

Postcard of The *Cell* from Museum of Science and Industry
Chicago, Illinois, Detail inside
c. 1959 Photograph by Vince Townsley
Used by permission of the Archives,
Museum of Science and Industry
Chicago, Illinois

Not since Otto Neurath's 1920's ISOTYPE work on public health interpretation in Vienna, and Herbert Bayer's innovative exhibition style of the 1930s in Germany, had there been such innovation in this kind of display. Burtin's *Cell* exhibit, completed in 1958, was the first in a series that would continue for thirteen years. The "Upjohn Cell" was a walk-in, three-dimensional array of tubing lights and color in which the viewer was able to physically enter a human blood cell, the basic unit of all life. The completed model accomplished at a glance what the combination of existing means of information had failed to do: it produced an immediate appreciation of a cell's logical structure and functioning. To this he added the element of visual attraction resulting from the qualities of forms, material, lights, and colors; all integrated toward a clear understanding of the whole.

In its publicity material, Upjohn characterized The *Cell* as an interpretative presentation of the fundamental unit of life. The basic aim of the exhibit was to improve the understanding of structures or processes essential to life and health for physicians, cytologists, and students. Its creation required a full year of research, collation of facts and surmises, design, and construction. No neurobiologist himself, Burtin relied upon expert advice from Dr. Wilder Penfield, an international expert on the brain from Canada, and other leading brain authorities, as well as Upjohn's special projects manager, Dr. A. Garrard MacLeod, and his staff.

Construction of The *Cell* Exhibit
c. 1957–1958
Photograph by Ezra Stoller © Esto
8 x 10 inches

The *Cell* nucleus *Right*
c. 1958–1959
Photograph by Ezra Stoller © Esto
10 x 8 inches

The *Cell* exhibit was representative of no particular body part but rather an abstraction of a cell portrayed as technically accurate as the knowledge and conjecture of cytologists could make it. As it symbolized a human red blood cell magnified more than 1,000,000 times, the whole structure measured 24 feet in diameter and 11½ feet high. It sat on a metal mirror in order to give the visitor the impression of being inside the organism, even at the center of it, when walked through and around it. The *Cell* was constructed of acrylic plastic tubing to simulate the cytoplasm or outer material. There were some 2,200 sections in the cytoplasmic configuration, measuring a total of 3,700 linear feet, with the 7,500 necessary joints connected by hand. Along the interior wall were displayed scale models of all the elements of the cell. The exhibit required novel solutions in construction: for example, the "chromosomes" were made from vacuum cleaner tubes covered by a fibrous material. The effect of pulsating motion was necessary to create an illusion of a living organism; this was accomplished by a controlled blue light which traveled around the base at fifteen rotations per minute, requiring over a mile of electric wiring to realize the effect. The *Cell* was built by The Displayers, Inc., an exhibit fabrication firm in New York.

The Upjohn *Cell* was first shown at the June 1958 annual meeting of the American Medical Association in San Francisco. Immediately a popular art, science, and design attraction, it was exhibited in New York, London, and Chicago. Its great popularity brought attention to both Burtin and Upjohn. A leading research scientist brought his advanced students to observe The *Cell*, and was impressed to realize that only a few minutes of experiencing the exhibit was equivalent to several weeks of classroom instruction. More than ten million people walked through the exhibit during its lifetime. It was seen on television programs and in newspapers throughout the world, and was included in biology textbooks. Feature articles appeared in magazines such as *Life* and *Scientific American* during and after the cell showings.

The *Cell* in minature model form with Upjohn logo in back
c. 1957–1958
Photograph by Ezra Stoller © Esto
4 x 5 inches
Used by permission of Pfizer, Inc.

Will Burtin and Dr. MacLeod inside The *Cell* exhibit

c. 1958, Photograph by Ted Russell for *Life* magazine, 17 x 11 inches

Industrial Design magazine reported that:

> The model does not "prove" anything, but it does imagine with great graphic inventiveness: the plastic shapes and forms evoke a surrealist world. In fact, because it was difficult conceiving in the round what no one yet has ever seen, Burtin found in surrealism a kind of unconscious, or prescient, visualization of some of the elements he needed for constructing the cell. So that although his model is based chiefly on medical slides and photomicrographs, it relates itself to (and visually corroborates) the weird and fantastic vocabulary of surrealism's imaginary shapes, making those once far-fetched and "unreal" images now appear tame, "real", and surprisingly natural—seeming demonstration, once again, that nature imitates art.[19]

The Upjohn *Cell* exhibit was a highlight of Burtin's professional life. During his forty-five year career, he pioneered the use of visual design to interpret and communicate science, but his large-scale three-dimensional presentations carried the design, craft, and art of communication and exhibit design to new heights.

19 Will Burtin
  "The Design of the Cell"
  Industrial Design magazine
  August, 1958, p. 59

Design Responsibility in the Age of Science

In their *Graphis* article, Burtin and Lessing concluded with a prophetic challenge to those involved in visualization:

> Much remains to be done in grappling with the task of bringing into human consciousness the new realities of relativistic physics, atomic structure, and their interrelations in such phenomena as cosmic radiation, atomic reactions, genetics and the like. With few exceptions the contemporary artist's grasp and understanding of space relations is too academic and inchoate yet to encompass this new vista opening before man's exploration of nature and himself. In the development of a greatly extended visual consciousness, the next stages of the arts need to be more and more occupied with these exciting tasks.[20]

Panel with The *Cell* exhibit
1959, Photograph by Ezra Stoller © Esto
8 x 10 inches

20 Will Burtin
 "The Design of the Cell"
 Industrial Design magazine
 August, 1958, p. 59

In his essay "Design Responsibility in an Age of Science," Will Burtin suggests that creativity in the hands of a designer or artist can unify the efforts between man and science. This, in turn, will establish a worthy environment, moving us toward a planned destiny. Recognition and acceptance of the social responsibility of design may make it one of the most valuable creative tools for the development of the first great adventure of all humans, the scientific culture.

Scope magazine cover
Volume 111, No. 8, Summer 1952
Used by permission of Pfizer, Inc.

21 Remington, R. Roger and Fripp, Robert S. P.
Design and Science
The Life and Work of Will Burtin
London: Lund Humphries, 2007

22 Morrissey, Jake
The Genius in the Design: Bernini, Borromini,
and the Rivalry that Transformed Rome
New York: Harper Collins, 2005, pp. 13–14

23 Henrion, F. H. K.
Unpublished obituary for Will Burtin, 1971
Will Burtin, Zurich: Alliance Graphique
Internationale, AGI pamphlet, c. 1972

In 1971, Burtin organized an exhibition at the American Institute of Graphic Arts in New York covering his work from the previous twenty years. It was described as "designs for mass communication in the science era—by Will Burtin"—and there was considerable evidence of his interest in visualization among the pieces on display. Among his contemporaries and with design historians today, Will Burtin was a pioneer in the subset of graphic design known as Information Design. His mature work was a bridge between science and the means of creating visual form that makes complex information simple and understandable. Burtin's son-in-law, Robert Fripp, wrote in 2007, "Burtin was to graphic design what Einstein was to physics."[21]

"But recognition of such men and their talents does not come without a price," as Jake Morrissey has written. "It is human nature to distrust genius. We are suspicious of the exceptional and the brilliant; they unsettle us. Too often we recoil at the extraordinary, alarmed by the originality we see. If we are not prepared for the canvas of a van Gogh or the poetry of a Blake, we're confused, even angry. It is a rare artist, a rare man, who can produce work that others welcome and that can weather the whimsy of taste and the scrutiny of time."[22] And so it was with Will Burtin. His friend and colleague F. H. K. Henrion summed it up best: "Before anyone else, he realised the need of science and scientific concepts and theories to be understood by people other than scientists, and he knew that only a designer who can talk to scientists would be in a position to put these concepts clearly and dramatically across."[23]

The *Cell* Exhibit on display
Photograph by Keturah Blakely
4 x 4 inches
Courtesy of Will Burtin Collection, RIT

The *Cell* Developmental sketches
3 x 4½ inches
Courtesy of Will Burtin Collection, RIT

Views on Visualization by Will Burtin

Assisted by urgent needs for a better understanding of complex problems in medical science and related researches, and supported by a progressive manufacturer, it became possible to select themes and to design educational models of some of the more significant structures and processes of life that had been revealed by science in recent years. The primary value of such models—as well as graphic design work preceding and following them—was that they reduced the time necessary for the study and understanding of a science problem. The secondary value consists in that they provide a physical and optical orientation which facilitates an intimate grasp of the inter-relatedness of all parts that make up for example—a basic cell—so important for the various chemical functions of the body on which life and health are based.

Will Burtin, *Design Responsibility in the Age of Science*, Burtin Collection, 12–13

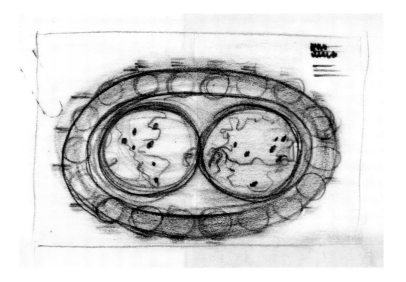

Once this overall grasp has been achieved, a student or doctor can remember the character of the whole structure in such a way that deviations from the normal—associated with disease—or the specialization of cells—for muscles, nerves, organs, skin, etc.—are understood. On this basis, the outcome of further specialized professional study of details which come to scientists in often confusingly specialized forms of charts, electron micrographs, direct microscopic observations, literature, x-ray diffraction photos or genetic or chemical tables, is greatly enhanced and results in increasing precision, and in real knowledge.

Will Burtin, *Design Responsibility in the Age of Science*, Burtin Collection, 13

Scope magazine covers
Volume IV, No. 9, 1956
Volume IV, No. 11, 1957 *Right*
Used by permission of Pfizer, Inc.

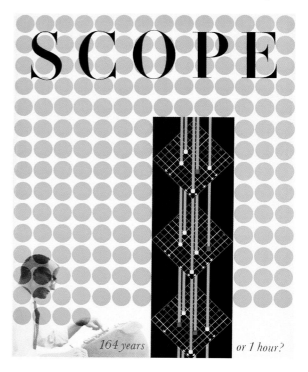

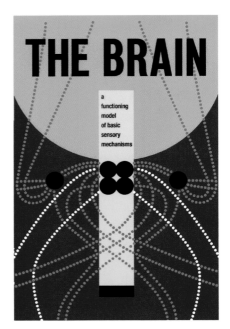

Brain Exhibit promotional poster
Designed by Will Burtin, 1960
36½ x 24 inches
Used by permission of Pfizer, Inc.

Building the Brain Exhibit *Right*
1960, Photograph by Jerry Cooke
8 x 10 inches
© The Jerry Cooke Archives, Inc.

Human imagination is limited by what we can have an image or "model" of. Such models are not necessarily related or limited to representational images in our minds. In communicating a thought we find that we have to project almost continuously images or image-related verbal symbols in order to achieve a situation in which a listener or an audience "sees"–that is, remembers– a semblance of what we project. Thereby the meaning of what we wish to be communicated can be understood.

Will Burtin, *Design Responsibility in the Age of Science*, Burtin Collection, 7

Will Burtin and colleagues
6 ⅜ x 8¼ inches
Courtesy of BBC Television Service

This condensation of abstract planning into concrete imagery
or projected models will have far-reaching consequences
for education and for the further exploration of what we can
think out, explore and explain.

Will Burtin, *Design Responsibility in the Age of Science*, Burtin Collection, 8

To convey meaning, to facilitate understanding of reality and
thereby help further progress, is a wonderful and challenging task
for design. The writer, scientist, painter, philosopher and the
designer of visual communication in commerce, are all partners
in the task of inventing the dramatic and electrifying shortcut
to a more comprehensive grasp of our time.

Will Burtin, "1920–1940–1960", Burtin Collection, 2

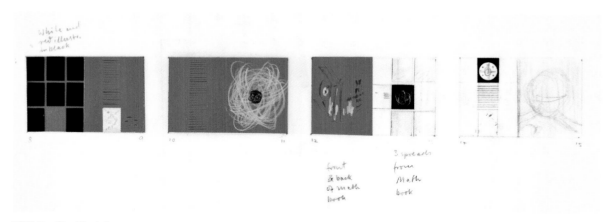

Will Burtin Sketch
Original sketch 9 x 12 inches
Courtesy of Will Burtin Collection, RIT

WILL BURTIN TIMELINE

Excerpted
with permission from
R. Roger Remington
and Robert S. P. Fripp
from
*Design and Science:
The Life and
Work of Will Burtin*
Vermont
Lund Humphries
2007

1908–1972	WILL BURTIN
1908	Born Cologne, Germany, to August and Gertrud Bürtin, January 27
1922	Studied typography at Handwerkskammer Köln (1922–26), and graphic and industrial design at the Kölner Werkschulen (from 1926) with Richard Riemerschmied and Jacob Erbar
1927–38	Opened design studio in Cologne, creating booklets, posters, type books, exhibitions, displays, advertising, and movies for German, French and other European clients
C 1931	While teaching in Berlin, met art student Hilde Munk
1932	Married Hilda Munk (1910–1960)
1937	Joseph Goebbels asked Burtin to become design director at the Propaganda Ministry; Burtin stalled for time; Hilde Munk Burtin wrote to her cousin Max Munk in Maryland, requesting his sponsorship into the United States
1938	Hitler repeated Goebbels' demand that Burtin become Propaganda Ministry's design director; Pressure to accept this post triggered hasty escape to the U.S.; Entry sponsored by Max Munk, aeronautics pioneer and inventor of the wind tunnel developer

1938	Burtin's first job in the U.S. was designing the *FlexOprop* logo, trademark of Munk Aeronautical Laboratory; Within months Burtin won a contract to design the Federal Works Exhibition for the U.S. Pavilion at the New York World's Fair
1939	Designed cover of *The Architectural Forum* magazine issue of the New York World's Fair; Established design practice in New York
1940	Designed booklet *Vesalius*, first project for The Upjohn Company
1939–43	Taught communication design at Pratt Institute, New York
1941	Awarded the New York Art Directors' Club medal; Designed his first *Scope* Magazine cover for Upjohn featuring a "test-tube baby" decades before the concept became a reality
1942	A-D magazine issue devoted to Burtin's work from 1930–40, featuring first work for Upjohn Company and *Fortune* magazine; The Burtins' only child, Carol, was born on October 10
1943–45	Drafted into U.S. Army, assigned to Office of Strategic Services (OSS); Designed "strategic subjects" presentations at OSS, Washington, DC Designed gunnery manuals for U.S. Air Force's aerial gunners
1945–49	*Fortune* magazine asked the Army to discharge Burtin and recruited him as Art Director; His contract permitted freelance work; Assignments for Upjohn and other clients grew in number
1948	Burtin's exhibition, *Integration: The New Discipline in Design,* ran at The Composing Room, New York. He continued major design work for The Upjohn Company, Kalamazoo, MI
1949	Burtin left *Fortune* magazine. Will Burtin Inc. rented offices at 11 West 42 Street. Graphis printed "Integration" as an article; Burtin teamed with writer Lawrence Lessing to describe the seminal wartime gunnery manuals project

1949–71	As design consultant for Upjohn, Burtin and a growing team created a new Upjohn text-only logo, establishing a unified design on all Upjohn packaging and printed materials in effect establishing corporate branding, an honor he shares with Lester Beall
C 1949	Director, American Institute of Graphic Arts (AIGA)
1949	Worked as a designer and consultant in advertising, industrial and editorial projects for clients such as Eastman Kodak Company, IBM, the Smithsonian Institution, Mead Paper, Union Carbide, Herman Miller Furniture Company, George Nelson Design, the United States Information Agency and several publishers; *Integration* exhibit at The Information Library, Chicago
1950s	Taught at Parsons School of Design and at Pratt Institute, NY James Marston Fitch, Editor, *The Architectural Forum* magazine appointed Burtin as design consultant to the magazine
1954	*Print* magazine featured Burtin and his work for Upjohn in an article, "A Program in Print: Upjohn and Design"
1955–56	Served with Saul Bass as program co-chair and speaker at the International Design Conference, Aspen, Colorado; Awarded the New York Art Directors' Club medal
C 1955	Will Burtin, Inc. moved offices to 132 East 58 Street
1957	Began design of walk-in *Cell* Exhibit for Upjohn Company; Designed a traveling exhibit, *Window on America* for the U.S. Information Agency, Kalamazoo, MI; also shown in Europe
1958	The *Cell* exhibit opened at the American Medical Asociation convention, gaining wide national and international attention; *Kalamazoo* was displayed in Berlin; Burtin returned from Zurich with a typeface that would later become named *Helvetica*

1959	Pratt Institute named Burtin Professor and Chair of the Department of Visual Communications; Burtin organized and chaired the *Typography USA* conference, New York; The *Cell* exhibit arrived in London to be televised for two science specials on the BBC television program, *What is Life?*
1960	Burtin's massive *Brain* exhibition for Upjohn anticipated "multi-media" by 30 years. Hilda Munk Burtin died on October 10, her daughter's 18th birthday
1961	Burtin's massive *Uranium Atom* exhibit opened in the lobby of the new Union Carbide building on Park Avenue; Burtin married art director and long-time family friend Cipe Pineles; Will and Carol Burtin moved to the Pineles' home in Stony Point, New York; The *Brain* toured major cities throughout Europe
1962	Designed a spread in *Comment 200* publication using Ezra Stoller's time-lapse photograph from the *Union Carbide Atom* exhibit; Burtin's touring *Visual Aspects of Science* exhibit and booklet featured work for clients: Kodak, IBM, Upjohn and Union Carbide
1963	Designed a large-scale *Metabolism* exhibit for Upjohn; The Royal College of Art, London, hosted an exhibition of Burtin's work
1964	Will Burtin, Inc. designed the Eastman Kodak pavilion and exhibit at the New York World's Fair, with film and slideshow by Saul Bass and Sy Wexler; Burtin designed the interior and the *Abraham Lincoln* exhibit for the Fair's Illinois State Pavilion, with a film by Saul Bass; and a multiple-projector slide exhibit for the Hall of Sciences, with Wexler and Bass; The *Brain* exhibit moved into the New York State pavilion

1965	Burtin organized and chaired the *Vision 65* Conference at Southern Illinois University, Carbondale, Illinois; Will Burtin, Inc. designed and fitted a large-scale lobby exhibit for Brunswick Corporation in Chicago; Burtin's essay "Design in Communication," was published in *Education of Vision*, Vision + Value Series, edited by Gyorgy Kepes
1966	Will Burtin, Inc. designed *Story of Mathematics for Young People,* a book set entirely in the typeface Helvetica for Pantheon; Upjohn released Burtin's *Genes in Action* exhibit (The Chromosome Puff) at the AMA convention; "Walk-in Portrait of a Gene at Work" article on Burtin's exhibits appeared in *Life* magazine, July 8
1967	Burtin organized and chaired the *Vision 67* Conference at New York University, New York; The Upjohn *Genes in Action* exhibit transformed into the *Heredity and You* exhibit for display to a lay audience in the lobby of the Time-Life Building, NY; Commissioned by James M. Fitch, Burtin developed new New York street signage
1968	Will Burtin, Inc. developed a signage system for the University Circle Development Foundation, Cleveland, Ohio
1969	Burtin's *Defense of Life* exhibit opened at the AMA convention in New York's Coliseum, with a film produced by Sy Wexler; Burtin designed the *Defense of Life* booklet and related materials
1970	The AIGA awarded Will Burtin a solo exhibit for the following year; Burtin proposed, and won preliminary acceptance for an exhibition called *The Biosphere*, for the United Nations Conference on the Human Environment (the Earth Summit), in Stockholm, 1972
1971	Harvard University appointed Burtin Research Fellow in Visual and Environmental Studies, Carpenter Center. His one-man AIGA exhibit, *The Communication of Knowledge*, opened in New York

1972	Will Burtin died on January 18, in Mount Sinai Hospital, NY; Saul Bass gave a eulogy at a memorial in New York; in September, the U.S. Embassy in London hosted a memorial exhibition
1973	Cipe Pineles adopted Carol Fripp
1989	R. Roger Remington and Dr. Barbara Hodik included a chapter on Burtin in *Nine Pioneers in American Graphic Design*, MIT Press. Chris Mullen developed a *Fortune* magazine database in the U.K.
1991	Following the death of Cipe Pineles, the unsorted archives of Pineles, Will Burtin and William Golden were deposited in the RIT archives; the Will Burtin collection was formally gifted in 2000
2005	Case study article on Burtin's *Brain* exhibit for Upjohn written by R. Roger Remington for *Information Design Journal*
2006	A Getty Foundation grant facilitated archival organization and rehousing of the Burtin collection at RIT
2007	*Design and Science: The Life and Work of Will Burtin* book written by R. Roger Remington and Robert S. P. Fripp published by Lund Humphries, London and Vermont, U.S.A.

COLOPHON

Design	Bruce Ian Meader and R. Roger Remington
Production	Molly Q. Cort and Marnie Soom
Typefaces	Sabon designed by Jan Tschichold and Frutiger designed by Adrian Frutiger
Paper	Blazer Silk
Printing	More Vang Alexandria, Virgina